To Mei Mei—my angel   —M. M.

To those who choose to follow their dreams
and make the world a better place   —J. R.

ATHENEUM BOOKS FOR YOUNG READERS • An imprint of Simon & Schuster Children's Publishing Division •
1230 Avenue of the Americas, New York, New York 10020 • Text copyright © 2018 by Michael James Mahin •
Illustrations copyright © 2018 by Jose Ramirez • All rights reserved, including the right of reproduction in whole or in
part in any form. • ATHENEUM BOOKS FOR YOUNG READERS is a registered trademark of Simon & Schuster, Inc.
Atheneum logo is a trademark of Simon & Schuster, Inc. • For information about special discounts for bulk purchases,
please contact Simon & Schuster Special Sales at 1-866-506-1949 or business@simonandschuster.com. • The Simon
& Schuster Speakers Bureau can bring authors to your live event. For more information or to book an event, contact
the Simon & Schuster Speakers Bureau at 1-866-248-3049 or visit our website at www.simonspeakers.com. • Book
design by Ann Bobco and Vikki Sheatsley • The text for this book was set in Brandon Grotesque. • The illustrations for
this book were rendered in acrylic and enamel markers on canvas. • Manufactured in China • 0618 SCP • First Edition •
10 9 8 7 6 5 4 3 2 1 • Library of Congress Cataloging-in-Publication Data • Names: Mahin, Michael James,
author. | Ramirez, Jose, illustrator. • Title: When angels sing : the story of Carlos Santana / Michael Mahin ; illustrated
by Jose Ramirez. • Description: First edition. | New York : Atheneum Books for Young Readers, [2018] •
Identifiers: LCCN 2017007274 • ISBN 9781534404137 (hardcover) • ISBN 9781534404144 (eBook) •
Subjects: LCSH: Santana, Carlos—Juvenile literature. | Rock musicians—United States—
Biography—Juvenile literature. • Classification: LCC ML3930.S26 M34 2018 |
DDC 787.87/164092 [B]—dc23• LC record available at
https://lccn.loc.gov/2017007274

WHEN ANGELS SING

The Story of Rock Legend Carlos Santana

MICHAEL MAHIN • Illustrated by JOSE RAMIREZ

Atheneum Books for Young Readers • New York London Toronto Sydney New Delhi

When you were born, your *tía abuela* called you *el cristalino*, the crystal one. She thought the light of angels shined through you.

Your father wanted to name you Geronimo, after the brave Apache freedom fighter. He was proud of his *mestizo* blood.

But your mother, as always, had the final word.

"Carlos."

Your father, like your grandfather before him, was a traveling musician.

You missed him when he went away. You missed the soapy smell of Maja on his skin and the smile in his eyes, but most of all you missed the sound of his violin.

When he was home, people would crowd the square to hear him play. It was a sound that filled the world with magic and love and feeling and healing. It was a sound that made angels real.

You wanted to make angels real too.

1952

First, you tried *el clarinete*, but the buzzy reed was too fussy for your nose. Then you tried *el corneo*, grandfather's instrument. But the taste of brass was too bitter on your lips.

Finally, you tried *el violín*. You scratched and squeaked and practiced so hard, your tears stained its wood. But it would not sing for you. Not like it sang for your father.

There were no angels when you played. Not yet, at least.

When I am good enough, they will come, you thought.

To you, life in Autlán de Navarro was *escondidas*, hide-and-seek, played beneath the mesquite trees with your brothers and sisters. It was the PLOP-POP of a red, ripe mango; the CROO-CROO of a chachalaca bird; and the BUBBLE-BOIL of *posole* on the stove.

On special days it was *biznagas*, sweets made from cactus, and *alfajor*, a kind of cookie made with *dulce de leche.*

But life without running water and electricity was hard. And when the nibble-sting of the *chinches* and *pulgas* became too much, your mother sold everything and took you to Tijuana.

1955

Tijuana wasn't much better. Sure, there were fresh *tamales* and *chiles rellenos* and the orangey *pipián* and chocolate-like *mole*, but Colonia Libertad was still the ghetto, and you were still so poor.

Soon, you were dressed like a *charro* and playing *tu violín* for fifty cents a song.

"'La Cucaracha!' 'Besame Mucho!'" they said.

Tourist music, you thought.

But it was a way to make money, so your father forced you to learn more songs. Mozart. Brahms. Polkas. Boleros. Gypsy music.

"You must put your heart into it!" he said.

You could not.

This is not the music my angels want to hear, you thought. *This is why they do not sing for me.*

1958

Your mother knew you loved music, even though you hated the violin. One day, she took you to Palacio de Municipal Park, with its bustling walkways and chiming carts.

You had heard the blues before, but you had never seen how the music was made. You had never seen someone play *la guitarra*. At least not like this.
The hair on your arms stood up.
An angel's breath? you thought.

Your father was away as usual, but your mother sent him a letter. After saving enough money, he sent home *una guitarra*. It was battered and bruised and beautiful.

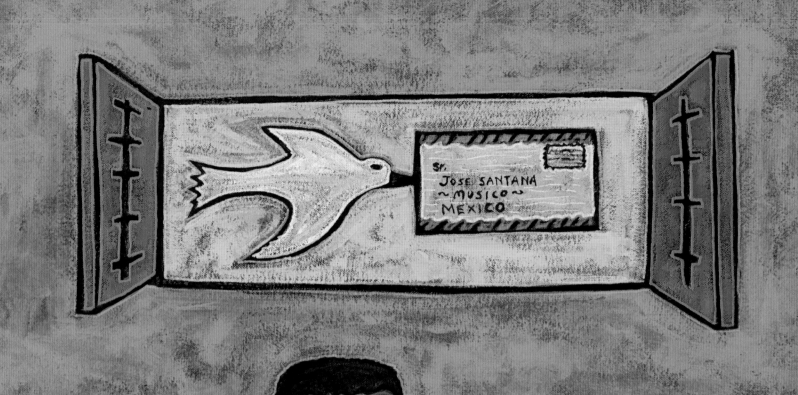

You found an old radio, took your guitar, and played along in a storage room in the dark because that was the only quiet place in the house. You closed your eyes and let your ears lead the way, and you taught yourself to follow the PLUNK of *el piano*, and the BOUNCE of *el bajo*, and the SWAY of *el saxofón*, and most importantly, the GROOVE of *la guitarra*.

You collected the ingredients and marinated your soul in them and learned that playing the blues was not about the color of your skin or which part of town you came from. It was about feeling the music.

You did not put your heart into it, like your father had said. Instead, you let the music put its heart into you.

Your family moved again. You liked your new house in San Francisco. You liked the running water and electricity. But riding the bus and going to school and making friends was hard. Especially because you didn't speak English.

They said, "Car antenna?"

And you said, "No. Car . . . los San . . . tana."

They called you a chili-bean eater. And gave you tests that you couldn't read. And held you back a year because they thought you were dumb.

1963

So you ran away. All the way back to Tijuana. Just you and *tu guitarra*.
My angels will come, you thought. And they will tell me I am good enough.
You watched TV and improved your English and learned how to respect a song and its melody.

But no angels came, and you started to wonder if they ever would.
Still, when your family came to find you, you did not want to go home.

San Francisco was a mess of music, just like the jukebox at Tick Tock Burgers, where you worked. You washed pots and mopped floors and started a blues band and listened to Willie Bobo and the Beatles and B.B. King while the smell of Clorox burned your nostrils and tried to bleach your soul white. But you wouldn't let it. Just like your father, you were proud of your *mestizo* blood.

1964

Your brother was living in the Central Valley. He was a *campesino*, working the fields. Like so many migrant workers, he suffered under the cruel, gear-crush of exploitation until Cesar Chavez and Dolores Huerta started fighting back. *¡Sí se puede!* they said. *Yes, we can.*

This helped your brother, and even though you weren't there, it helped you, too, deep in your soul.

If they can, I can, you thought.

So you kept playing. And practicing. And searching for your sound.

One day, you went to Aquatic Park. *Las congas* rumbled into your chest.

There was magic in their beat. A breath. A breeze. A feeling. The breaking dawn of something the world had never seen before. And this tu-TOOMA tocka-tocka-tock, tu-TOOMA tocka-tocka-tock was the beat of its heart.

Maybe this is the music that will make my angels sing, you thought.

So you took the soul of the blues, and the brains of jazz, and the energy of rock and roll. And to that, you added the slow heat of Afro-Cuban drums and the cilantro-scented sway of the music you'd grown up with.

1966

There were a lot of bands in San Francisco, but none were playing music like that. There was something electric in the air, and its name was the Santana Blues Band.

Soon, everyone knew who you were. Everyone came to see you. Everyone, except your angels.

Will I ever be good enough? you wondered.

You were getting too old to believe in angels anyway.

All around you, the nurturing light of possibility was beginning to glow. Martin Luther King Jr. was changing the world, and young people like you were too. You were taking your hearts and coloring them open and making the world a better place.

1968

And then . . . the light was gone. *He* was gone.
In the background, the bombs of Vietnam grew
louder and louder. Suddenly, it was as if hate and fear
had covered the world in darkness.

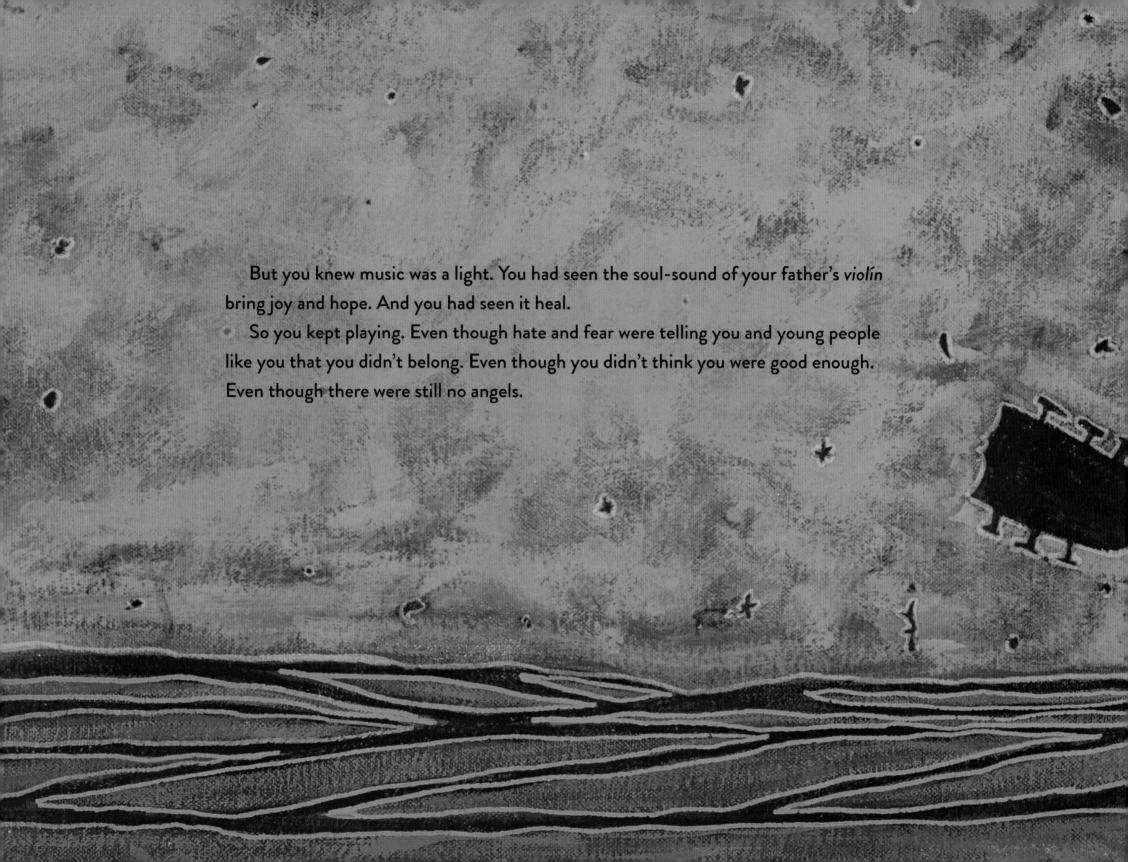

But you knew music was a light. You had seen the soul-sound of your father's *violín* bring joy and hope. And you had seen it heal.

So you kept playing. Even though hate and fear were telling you and young people like you that you didn't belong. Even though you didn't think you were good enough. Even though there were still no angels.

The Santana Blues Band was big in San Francisco. But there in New York, at the muddy Woodstock music festival, you were unknown. Unsteady. And scared.
But on that day, in front of more than 400,000 people you didn't know, you took the stage anyway.

You looked out into the audience, hoping for a miracle. Hoping for something to tell you
that you were good enough. Hoping you had been wrong to stop believing in angels.
But there were no angels out there. There had never been angels *out* there.
And suddenly you knew why.

You took the stage,
and you stopped looking *out*,
and you started looking *in*.
And, at last, you heard your angels sing.

author's note

On the heels of his career-making performance at Woodstock, Carlos Santana became an international music star.

Before "world music" was even a musical genre, Santana pioneered a unique sound that fused American blues, rock, and jazz traditions with the sound and feel of Latin American and African music. Santana's band, like his music, was always multicultural.

Despite last-minute permit issues, rain, sound system malfunctions, and a host of other problems, the Woodstock Music and Art Fair was a resounding success. Attended by more than 400,000 people and host to performances by the likes of music legends Jimi Hendrix, The Band, Sly & the Family Stone, and Janis Joplin, it endures as a defining moment in American cultural and music history. Today, it is considered the symbolic peak of the counter-cultural movement of the 1960s.

Shortly after Woodstock, the band, which had changed its name to just "Santana," released its first album. This album gave birth to the hit single "Evil Ways" and would eventually go double platinum after selling more than two million copies. Thirty years later, at the 1999 Grammy Awards, Santana's album *Supernatural* was nominated in nine categories, including Album of the Year, Record of the Year, and Song of the Year. It won in every category, tying the record for most Grammy Awards received in a single year.

In 2009, Santana received a Lifetime Achievement Award at the Billboard Latin Music Awards. And in 2013, he was invited by President Barack Obama to the White House, where he received one of the highest honors a performing artist can receive in the United States: a Kennedy Center Honor.

Carlos Santana believes that we each carry the spark of the divine within us and that we each, in our own way, have the power to heal the world. With this in mind, Santana founded the Milagro Foundation to benefit vulnerable children around the world by making grants to community-based organizations in the areas of education, health, and the arts.

bibliography

Santana, Carlos, with Ashley Kahn and Hal Miller. *The Universal Tone: Bringing My Story to Light.* New York: Little, Brown, 2014.

Shapiro, Marc. *Carlos Santana: Back on Top.* New York, St. Martin's, 2002.

Leng, Simon. *Soul Sacrifice: The Santana Story.* Ontario: Firefly Publishing, 2001.

further listening

Santana (Columbia, 1969)

Abraxas (Columbia, 1970)

Supernatural (Arista, 1999)

The Essential Santana (Sony, 2002)

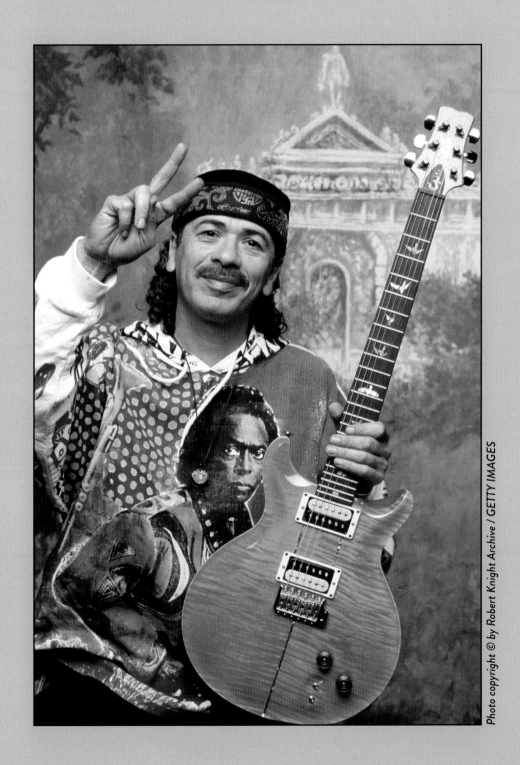